STEM IN THE REAL WORLD

COMPUTER SCIENCE
IN THE REAL WORLD

by Lisa Idzikowski

Content Consultant
Jeffrey Miller
Associate Professor of Engineering Practice
Department of Computer Science
University of Southern California

Core Library

An Imprint of Abdo Publishing
abdopublishing.com

abdopublishing.com

Published by Abdo Publishing, a division of ABDO, PO Box 398166, Minneapolis, Minnesota 55439. Copyright © 2016 by Abdo Consulting Group, Inc. International copyrights reserved in all countries. No part of this book may be reproduced in any form without written permission from the publisher. Core Library™ is a trademark and logo of Abdo Publishing.

Printed in the United States of America, North Mankato, Minnesota
092015
012016

**THIS BOOK CONTAINS
RECYCLED MATERIALS**

Cover Photo: Michael Bowles/Rex Features/AP Images
Interior Photos: Michael Bowles/Rex Features/AP Images, 1; Kim Kulish/Corbis, 4; iStockphoto, 8 (top), 10, 34, 45; ifixit.com, 8 (bottom); Bettmann/Corbis, 12, 15, 19; NLM/Science Source/ Getty Images, 17; Science and Society Picture Library/Getty Images, 22, 43; Jan Woitas/Picture-Alliance/DPA/AP Images, 24; Chris Schmidt/iStockphoto, 27; Evan Vucci/AP Images, 28; Red Line Editorial, 31; Alan Altman/Bettmann/Corbis, 32; Volker Steger/Science Source, 37; Zhang Yu/Imaginechina/AP Images, 39

Editor: Arnold Ringstad
Series Designer: Ryan Gale

Library of Congress Control Number: 2015945539

Cataloging-in-Publication Data
Idzikowski, Lisa.
 Computer science in the real world / Lisa Idzikowski.
   p. cm. -- (STEM in the real world)
 ISBN 978-1-68078-040-6 (lib. bdg.)
 Includes bibliographical references and index.
 1. Computer science--Juvenile literature.   I. Title.
 004--dc23
                                                                 2015945539

CONTENTS

CHAPTER ONE
Computers in
the Real World 4

CHAPTER TWO
The History of Computers 12

CHAPTER THREE
Computer Careers 24

CHAPTER FOUR
The Future of Computers 34

Fast Facts 42

Stop and Think 44

Glossary 46

Learn More..........................47

Index 48

About the Author 48

COMPUTERS IN THE REAL WORLD

An artist sits at a computer. She taps on the keyboard. She clicks the mouse. Suddenly a colorful cartoon movie begins playing. An animated character leaps through a dazzling world. Shimmering water, bright sunlight, and lush trees appear. Then the movie stops. It has taken the artist days to create just a few seconds of this animated movie. She is a member of a huge team.

Computer animators use a variety of digital tools to make cartoon movies.

Computer Animation

Computer power combines with talented people to make incredible animated films. First the team writes a script. Then voice actors record their lines. Finally the computer team builds the movie's three-dimensional world. Animators create lifelike characters and amazing visual effects. The 1995 film *Toy Story* was the first feature-length computer-generated animated movie.

Together they are building the latest cartoon blockbuster one click at a time. Animation is one of many exciting fields that involve computers. Workers create characters and environments. They make them move realistically onscreen. They may have to figure out how wind affects blades of grass or strands of hair. It is a long process. But the results can be amazing. It is possible thanks to modern computers.

Inside Your Computer

Computers are devices that carry out instructions. They come in many shapes and sizes. Some have parts that are designed for their specific uses. But most computers have several parts in common.

The core of a computer is its central processing unit (CPU). The CPU is a computer chip containing many transistors. A transistor controls the flow of electricity. It allows the chip to carry out instructions. A single CPU may contain billions of transistors.

Computers also have memory. There are two main types of memory. Random-access memory (RAM) is used for short-term storage. Drives are used for long-term storage. They may be hard drives, solid-state drives, or USB drives. Both types of memory store instructions and data. They also store the results of those instructions.

Input and output devices allow people to interact with computers. Keyboards, mice, and cameras are input devices. Speakers, monitors, and printers are output devices.

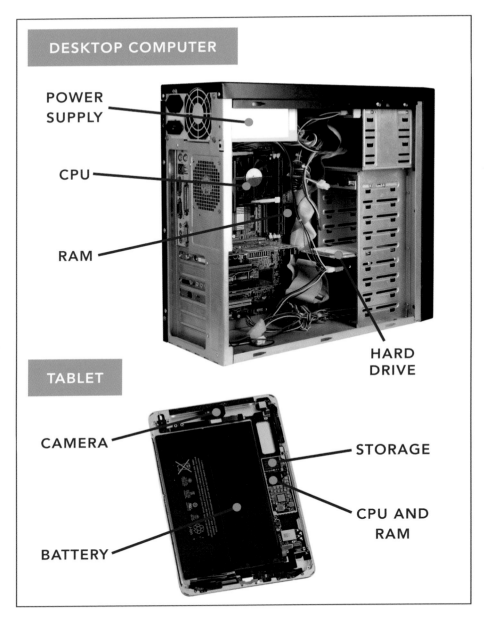

DESKTOP COMPUTER

POWER SUPPLY

CPU

RAM

HARD DRIVE

TABLET

CAMERA

STORAGE

CPU AND RAM

BATTERY

Computer Parts

These images show the various parts of a desktop computer and a tablet. What do you notice about them? How do the computers differ? How are they the same?

Computers All Around

Every day people use computers in schools, at homes, and at jobs. Computers help them read, write, drive, and play. They even help complete household chores. Computers are everywhere. It may seem as though they have always been around. But that is not the case. Computers have gone through decades of design and development. Personal computers (PCs) did not become widely available until the 1980s. Smartphones and tablets appeared only within the last decade.

Many ordinary things function with the help of computer chips. Today's cars, refrigerators, washing machines, and coffeemakers rely on them. In the future, computers will become an

Computers in Everyday Objects

Many of us use cell phones, laptops, and tablets. They make our lives safer, easier, and more fun. But what about all the other things you use every day? Microwaves, watches, televisions, toasters, cameras, and many other items have computer chips in them.

The tablets and other devices we use today are relatively recent inventions.

even more important part of daily life. This is why it is important that people learn how to use them. Many careers of the future will revolve around studying, designing, programming, and using computers.

Bill Gates founded the computer company Microsoft with Paul Allen in 1975. He began writing software when he was thirteen years old. In 2015 he wrote a letter to Microsoft employees talking about the history and future of computers:

> Early on, Paul Allen and I set the goal of a computer on every desk and in every home. It was a bold idea and a lot of people thought we were out of our minds to imagine it was possible. It is amazing to think about how far computing has come since then, and we can all be proud of the role Microsoft played in that revolution.
>
> Today though, I am thinking much more about Microsoft's future than its past. I believe computing will evolve faster in the next 10 years than it ever has before. We already live in a multi-platform world, and computing will become even more pervasive. We are nearing the point where computers and robots will be able to see, move and interact naturally, unlocking many new applications and empowering people even more.

Source: Ina Fried. "Here's the E-Mail Bill Gates Sent Commemorating Microsoft's Fortieth Birthday." Re/Code. Re/Code, April 3, 2015. Web. Accessed July 27, 2015.

Point of View

Bill Gates is speaking as a major figure in the computer industry. How might this affect his point of view about computer issues? Do you agree with his predictions about the future?

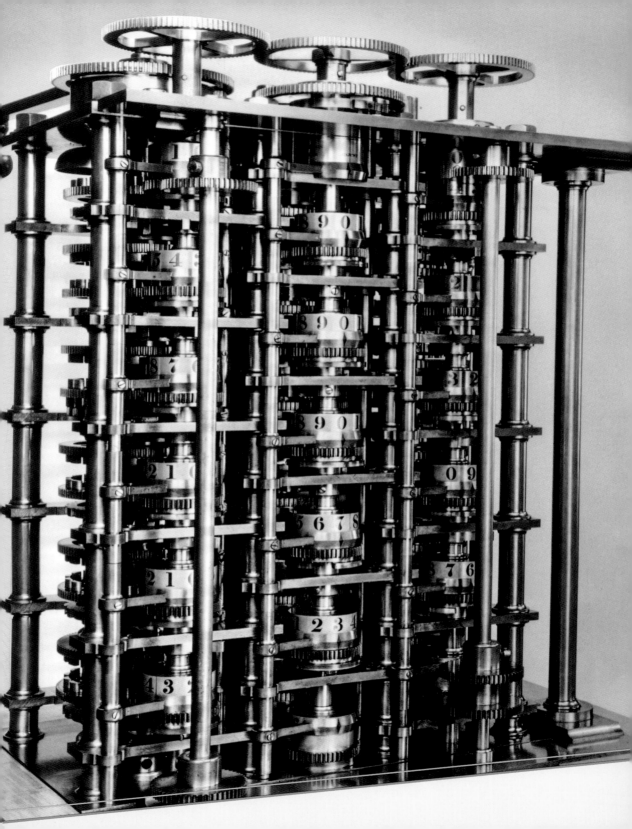

THE HISTORY OF COMPUTERS

Human beings have always counted things. At first they used their fingers. Later they began using other objects, such as pebbles. Eventually ancient people developed simple tools for counting and making calculations.

Over the centuries, calculations became more difficult. People were using math for complex scientific studies. They wanted to track the movement

Early computers were huge and made up of mechanical parts.

of the planets and predict the path of artillery shells. Scientists realized that some kind of machine was needed to speed up the process of calculations.

Early Calculating Machines

Gears, wheels, and cogs formed several of the first mechanical calculating machines. In 1642 Blaise Pascal built a machine that could add and subtract. His calculating machine was the first one ever demonstrated in public. Mathematician Gottfried Leibniz later improved Pascal's design. He constructed a machine that could add, subtract, multiply, and divide.

Mathematician Charles Babbage designed two calculating machines in the early 1800s. They were the Difference Engine and the more advanced Analytical Engine. Neither was built during Babbage's lifetime. Yet Babbage is recognized for his pioneering designs. He is sometimes called the "grandfather of the modern computer."

Babbage was a pioneer in the history of computing.

The Age of Electrical Machines

The United States has conducted a census every ten years since 1790. By the late 1800s, the population of the United States had greatly increased. It took an extremely long time to organize the data from millions of people around the country. The American Census Bureau offered a prize for anyone with a solution to the problem.

Herman Hollerith believed he had the answer. He created an electric machine. It processed information using holes in hand-punched cards. These holes represented the information people gave in response to the census questions. Hollerith earned the prize. His machine organized the census information quicker than before.

Thomas Edison and other scientists experimented with electricity during this time. Edison discovered that electric current could flow through glass tubes. These vacuum tubes turned on and off. They worked like switches and created signals. Vacuum tubes

Hollerith's machine could quickly count and summarize information.

made electrical computers possible. The resulting computers were much faster than older mechanical versions.

The Giants

Scientists developed the first electrical computers by the 1940s. These machines filled spaces the size of whole rooms. In the United Kingdom, engineers constructed the Colossus. It was designed to break secret codes during World War II (1939–1945).

The United States also built gigantic computers during the war. The Electronic Numerical Integrator and Computer (ENIAC) was completed in 1945. It weighed 30 tons (27 metric tons). The machine used 18,000 vacuum tubes. The Mark I was another giant US computer.

Computer use branched out from the military after the war. The television network CBS used a UNIVAC computer to predict the winner of the 1952 presidential election. Its operators fed it data from opinion polls. UNIVAC correctly guessed Dwight D. Eisenhower would be elected president.

These giant computers advanced computer science. But vacuum tubes had problems. They easily

Problem Solvers

Before 1945 the word *computer* meant a person who solved equations or math problems. Large teams of computers worked on major scientific projects. After World War II, the term was used to describe the machines that solved equations.

The computers of the 1940s and 1950s were enormous.

broke and burned out. A new innovation was needed to create the next generation of computers.

Transistors and Circuits

Two inventions pushed computer development ahead in the late 1940s. The first was the transistor, a substitute for the vacuum tube. Scientists joined silicon, a metal that conducts electricity, with plastic. They shaped the materials into a small device called a transistor. Engineers could combine multiple transistors into a single unit. This became known as the integrated circuit, or microchip. Using microchips, computers shrank in size. They also worked more quickly. These early integrated circuits are the ancestors of today's CPUs.

Scientists and engineers kept experimenting with this new technology. Another giant leap forward occurred in the early 1970s. Engineers developed an advanced integrated circuit called a microprocessor. All of a computer's functions could now be combined onto a single small chip.

Computers at that time were mainly used by scientists, engineers, and governments. Huge computers sat in rooms at universities and computer companies. Few thought the general public would use computers. The microprocessor soon changed that.

Personal Computers

In January 1975, the cover of *Popular Electronics* magazine advertised a personal computer called the Altair 8800. It did not include a screen or a keyboard. Users had to build the computer themselves from a kit. Today the Altair 8800 is hardly recognizable as a computer. But people were very excited about it. They realized the personal

Writing Software

Computers are only useful if they are running useful software. Software is the set of instructions that the computer follows. A piece of software is also known as a computer program. People write these programs in specialized computer languages. The programs are formatted in a certain way so that the computer can understand them.

The Altair 8800 was one of the earliest personal computers.

computer would allow them to write and use their own software at home.

The Computer Revolution Begins

Many personal computers became available within the next few years. These models included keyboards, screens, and other parts. Bill Gates and Paul Allen started Microsoft. Steve Jobs and Steve

Wozniak started Apple Computer. They wanted to bring computers and software to regular people. Computers got smaller and more powerful. By the 1990s, most people in the United States had used a computer. The development of the Internet and the World Wide Web made personal computers even more useful. People could send e-mail, search for information, and play games online. By the year 2000, the computer was an important part of everyday life.

FURTHER EVIDENCE

Chapter Two contains information about the history of computers. What was one main point of the chapter? What evidence supports this point? Read the article at the website listed below. What new information about the history of computers can you find?

1976: Apple Releases Its First Computer
mycorelibrary.com/computer-science

COMPUTER CAREERS

People use computers daily. Video games, social media, and even schoolwork depend on computer technology. This field is also known as information technology (IT). Information technology workers solve problems using computers.

These are not the only computer science jobs. Computer researchers work at universities, in the government, and for corporations. They create

Computer scientists work with the most advanced computer technology available.

smaller, faster computer chips. They also develop new programming languages. Their research pushes the field forward.

Software Engineering

Software engineers design and write computer programs. They are sometimes called programmers or coders. Many industries hire software engineers. One person might create programs for a power plant. Another might work on the latest video game. A software engineer might build a smartphone app or a website.

The field will grow as computer programs become more important to everyday life. Software engineers are in high demand. The first step

Education

Most IT jobs require some college education. To prepare for this, students should take classes in math and physics. Learning how to program is also extremely useful. There are free online classes on programming. Students should also take classes in English and language arts. Computer professionals need to be able to communicate their ideas clearly.

Computer programming is a valuable skill in today's world.

to becoming one is earning a college degree in computer science. Software engineers are usually well paid. The median salary is approximately $93,000 per year.

Hardware Engineering

Hardware engineers design new CPUs, memory chips, and other computer parts. They help make computers faster and more functional. They team up with software engineers to make sure hardware and software will work together properly.

President Barack Obama spoke about the importance of cybersecurity in a February 2015 speech.

Hardware engineers go to college and complete a four-year degree, usually in computer engineering. Wages in this field are fairly high. The median salary is around $100,000 a year.

Cybersecurity

One of the most important fields within IT is cybersecurity. Millions of computers around the world are connected to the Internet. This includes computers with sensitive information, such as military intelligence and bank accounts. Some people, known as hackers, try to break into these computer systems and steal information.

Cybersecurity workers defend against these attacks. They design, test, and install software to block hackers. Jobs in information security are among the fastest-growing computer careers. Workers usually get a college degree in computer science or information technology. They may take extra classes in cybersecurity. Their median pay is approximately $85,000.

Computer Science

Computer scientists do basic research on hardware and software. They study physics to know how electricity behaves within computer chips. They explore ways to make chips faster and more efficient. Computer scientists also work on new programming languages. They figure out how to improve the instructions they give to computers. This makes it possible for the computers to solve problems more quickly.

Just like other kinds of scientists, computer scientists run experiments to test their research. They publish the results in scientific journals. Hardware and software

Programming Languages

Different programming languages are written for different purposes. The language JavaScript is mainly used to create web pages. Apps for smartphones are usually written in Objective-C, Swift, or Java. Software engineers may use more than ten languages in their jobs.

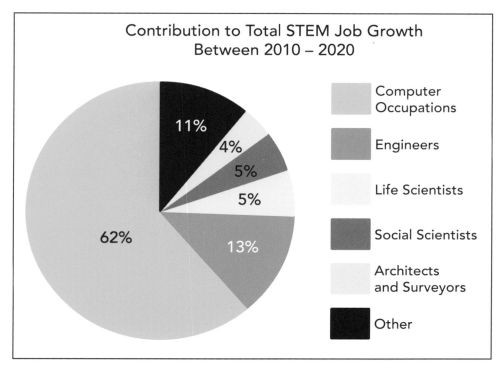

Contribution to Total STEM Job Growth Between 2010 – 2020

- Computer Occupations — 62%
- Engineers — 13%
- Life Scientists — 5%
- Social Scientists — 5%
- Architects and Surveyors — 4%
- Other — 11%

Job Growth in STEM Fields

Computer professions are expected to be one of the largest areas of job growth in Science, Technology, Engineering, and Math (STEM) fields. Compare and contrast the different types of careers shown in the graph. How does this demonstrate the importance of learning about computers now to prepare for the future?

engineers use these results when designing new computers.

To become a computer scientist, a person needs to earn a PhD in computer science. The median pay is approximately $102,000.

Grace Hopper rose to the rank of Rear Admiral in the US Navy before she retired in 1986 at the age of 79.

Computer Pioneers

There have been many important figures in computer history. Among these was Grace Murray Hopper, born in 1906. She graduated from college with degrees in math and physics. She then became a college math professor. She worked at Harvard University. Her team there developed the first programmable computer. Hopper's work led to the programming language COBOL, which is still in use today.

Alan Turing also played a key role in computer history. Born in 1912, he was an early pioneer in computer science and artificial intelligence. Turing worked for the British government during World War II. He helped crack codes. This shortened the war and saved many lives. Turing's story was told in the 2014 film *The Imitation Game.*

Bill Gates, born in 1955, helped bring personal computers to the masses. His company Microsoft made an operating system called Windows. By the 1990s, millions of computers around the world used Windows.

EXPLORE ONLINE

Chapter Three highlights Grace Hopper as an important figure in computer history. The website below provides additional information about her. What new information can you find on the website?

The World's First Computer Bug

mycorelibrary.com/computer-science

CHAPTER FOUR

THE FUTURE OF COMPUTERS

Computer technology advances at an amazing rate. Today's smartphones are much more powerful than the desktop computers of ten years ago. This pace seems likely to continue into the future.

Computer scientists are working on incredible new developments. One of the most promising is quantum computing. This technology may allow us

The computers we can wear on our wrists today are much faster than the computers that filled entire rooms in the 1950s.

to create much faster computers than ever before. Another major area of study is artificial intelligence. This work is helping make computers smarter.

The connections between computers are another important part of the future of computer science. More kinds of devices are connected to the Internet each year. Experts call this the "Internet of Things." These connections could help change our everyday lives.

Quantum Computing

The next generation of technology may involve quantum computers. Quantum computers do not rely on transistors and electricity. They take advantage of the behavior of tiny molecules and atoms. This would allow computers to be smaller and faster.

Researchers have created simple quantum computers in their labs. However, there is still much work to be done. The challenge is controlling the tiny parts that make up a quantum computer. It is very

Today's quantum computers are found only in high-tech laboratories.

difficult to examine these particles without changing them.

Artificial Intelligence

Another area of research is artificial intelligence. Researchers are building computers that work more like the human brain. This technology could have many uses. Smart robots could drive our cars, clean our homes, or even keep us company.

Many smartphones have simple versions of artificial intelligence. Users can ask a question and receive an answer. Artificial intelligence could change the way we interact with computers. It could be combined with

Making Quantum Computers

Research in quantum computers is complicated, expensive, and difficult. Some universities are teaming up with corporations to make this research happen. The University of Southern California is working with defense company Lockheed Martin. They are trying to bring quantum computers from laboratories to real-world use.

Virtual reality headsets use small screens and special lenses to let users feel like they are in a virtual world.

virtual reality headsets to create totally immersive, realistic worlds.

The Internet of Things

The Internet of Things will have a major impact on everyday life. Imagine a world in which your lawn knows it is getting too long. It sends a signal telling your robot lawn mower to trim it. Or consider a fridge that can tell it is low on eggs. It sends a reminder to

Sensors

One critical technology in the Internet of Things is sensors. These computer input devices collect information about their environment. For example, a smart lawn must be able to sense how long it is. Experts imagine a future when bridges will have sensors to detect ice or cracking concrete. This can help keep drivers safe and prevent bridge collapses.

your smartphone telling you to buy more. These kinds of connections between devices could make people's lives easier.

Computers have come a long way in just a few decades. In the 1950s, they were giant machines that took up rooms. Today a powerful computer can fit inside a wristwatch. And this is just the beginning. There are many promising advances on the horizon. The students of today will become the pioneering computer scientists of tomorrow.

Danelle Cline is a software engineer for the Monterey Bay Aquarium Research Institute in California. She explains that being a software engineer does not mean that you will be sitting in an office all day long:

> I work closely with scientists from different disciplines to design and build software to help them better understand the ocean. I don't sit at my desk all day like a lot of engineers do. I do spend time working from my computer and in meetings, but I also get to go to sea to make sure ocean-going projects I've completed work properly. When we go to sea, anything can happen and equipment can break. We joke that if you don't want your things to break, don't put them in the ocean! But it's a lot of fun.

> Source: Danielle Caldwell. "Danelle Cline, Software Engineer with Monterey Bay Aquarium Research Institute." STEM Works. STEM Works, January 29, 2013. Web. Accessed July 27, 2015.

Consider Your Audience

Adapt this passage for a different audience, such as your parents. Write a blog post conveying this same information for the new audience. How does your post differ from the original text and why?

- Computers are machines that carry out instructions. They have many parts, including CPUs, RAM, storage, and input and output devices, that let them complete these tasks and interact with users.

- The earliest electric computers date to the 1940s. They used vacuum tubes.

- Transistors and microchips revolutionized the world of computers, making them smaller, cheaper, and more powerful.

- The first personal computers were sold in the 1970s. Today almost everyone has used a computer.

- Software engineers design and write computer programs. Hardware engineers design and build the physical parts that make up computers.

- Computer scientists do the basic research that underlies the work of hardware and software engineers.

- Quantum computing and artificial intelligence are major areas of study for today's computer scientists.

STOP AND THINK

Say What?

Studying computers and computer science can mean learning a lot of new vocabulary. Find five words in this book you've never heard before. Use a dictionary to find out what they mean. Then write the meanings in your own words, and use each word in a new sentence.

Why Do I Care?

You may not know how to write computer programs, but you probably use them every day. With an adult's help, do some research on these programs. Who wrote them? What languages are they written in? How do the programs affect your daily life?

You Are There

This book discusses quite a bit of information about computers. Imagine you are writing a letter to a friend who is asking whether she should study computers. What would you tell her about computer careers? Be sure to include details in your letter.

Surprise Me

Chapter Two discusses the history of computers. What two or three facts about the history of computers surprised you? Write a few sentences about each fact. Why did you find each of these facts surprising?

GLOSSARY

artificial intelligence (AI)
a branch of computer science in which scientists aim to develop the ability for computers to learn and think

hacker
a person who breaks into a computer system to steal information

integrated circuit
many transistors combined together on a chip of silicon

memory
the parts of a computer that store information

microprocessor
a chip that contains the brains of the computer

operating system
a software program that helps other programs work with the computer's hardware

quantum computing
computer technology that uses the behavior of atoms and molecules to function

software
the set of instructions that a computer follows

transistor
an electronic part that controls the flow of electricity

vacuum tubes
glass tubes that can control the flow of electricity

LEARN MORE

Books

Computer. New York: DK Publishing, 2011.

Sande, Warren, and Carter Sande. *Hello World!: Computer Programming for Kids and Other Beginners.* Shelter Island, NY: Manning, 2014.

Websites

To learn more about STEM in the Real World, visit **booklinks.abdopublishing.com**. These links are routinely monitored and updated to provide the most current information available.

Visit **mycorelibrary.com** for free additional tools for teachers and students.

INDEX

Altair 8800, 21
artificial intelligence, 33, 36, 38

Babbage, Charles, 14

calculating machines, 14
computer animation, 5–6
computer scientists, 30–31, 35, 40
CPUs, 7, 8, 20, 27
cybersecurity, 29

ENIAC, 18

Gates, Bill, 11, 22, 33

hardware engineers, 27, 29
Hollerith, Herman, 16
Hopper, Grace Murray, 32–33

integrated circuits, 20
Internet, 23, 29, 36
Internet of Things, 36, 39–40

Jobs, Steve, 22

Leibniz, Gottfried, 14

memory
  drives, 7, 8
  RAM, 7, 8
microprocessors, 20–21

programming
  languages, 21, 26, 30, 32

quantum computing, 35–38

software engineers, 26–27, 30, 41

transistors, 7, 20–21, 36
Turing, Alan, 33

UNIVAC, 18

vacuum tubes, 16, 18, 20

World War II, 17, 18, 33

ABOUT THE AUTHOR

Before becoming a Library Youth Educator, Lisa Idzikowski taught elementary school. She and her family live in Wisconsin. Lisa writes books and articles about science and scientists, gardening, animals, nature, and history.